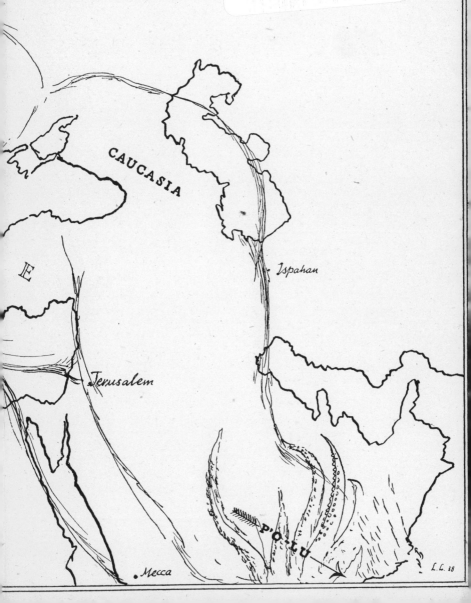

CAUCASIA

E

Ispahan

Jerusalem

P'OLU

Mecca

L.C. 18

TALIESSIN THROUGH LOGRES

TALIESSIN THROUGH LOGRES

by

CHARLES WILLIAMS

GEOFFREY CUMBERLEGE

OXFORD UNIVERSITY PRESS

LONDON   NEW YORK   TORONTO

Oxford University Press, Amen House, London E.C.4

EDINBURGH GLASGOW NEW YORK TORONTO MELBOURNE
WELLINGTON BOMBAY CALCUTTA MADRAS CAPE TOWN

Geoffrey Cumberlege, Publisher to the University

First published 1938
Second impression 1948

Printed in Great Britain

FOR

HUMPHREY MILFORD
UNDER WHOM WE OBSERVED
AN APPEARANCE OF
BYZANTIUM

CONTENTS

PRELUDE   I

TALIESSIN'S RETURN TO LOGRES   3

THE VISION OF THE EMPIRE   6

THE CALLING OF ARTHUR   14

MOUNT BADON   16

THE CROWNING OF ARTHUR   19

TALIESSIN'S SONG OF THE UNICORN   22

BORS TO ELAYNE ; THE FISH OF BROCELIANDE   24

TALIESSIN IN THE SCHOOL OF THE POETS   27

TALIESSIN ON THE DEATH OF VIRGIL   31

THE COMING OF PALOMIDES   33

LAMORACK AND THE QUEEN MORGAUSE OF ORKNEY   38

BORS TO ELAYNE ; ON THE KING'S COINS   42

THE STAR OF PERCIVALE   46

THE ASCENT OF THE SPEAR   48

THE SISTER OF PERCIVALE   51

THE SON OF LANCELOT   54

PALOMIDES BEFORE HIS CHRISTENING   64

THE COMING OF GALAHAD   69

THE DEPARTURE OF MERLIN   75

THE DEATH OF PALOMIDES   78

PERCIVALE AT CARBONEK   81

THE LAST VOYAGE   84

TALIESSIN AT LANCELOT'S MASS   89

NOTE   95

Unde est, quod non operatio propria propter
essentiam, sed haec propter illam habet ut
sit.

De Monarchia, I, iii.

Prelude

I

Recalcitrant tribes heard;
orthodox wisdom sprang in Caucasia and Thule;
the glory of the Emperor stretched to the ends of the world.

In the season of midmost Sophia
the word of the Emperor established a kingdom in Britain;
they sang in Sophia the immaculate conception of wisdom.

Carbonek, Camelot, Caucasia,
were gates and containers, intermediations of light;
geography breathing geometry, the double-fledged Logos.

II

The blind rulers of Logres
nourished the land on a fallacy of rational virtue;
the seals of the saints were broken; the chairs of the Table
    reeled.

Galahad quickened in the Mercy;
but history began; the Moslem stormed Byzantium;
lost was the glory, lost the power and kingdom.

Call on the hills to hide us
lest, men said in the City, the lord of charity
ride in the starlight, sole flash of the Emperor's glory.

I

III

Evil and good were twins
once in the alleys of Ispahan ; the Moslem
crying *Alla il Alla* destroyed the dualism of Persia.

Caucasia fell to the Moslem ;
the mamelukes seized the ancient cornland of Empire.
Union is breached ; the imams stand in Sophia.

Good is God, the muezzin
calls, but lost is the light on the hills of Caucasia,
glory of the Emperor, glory of substantial being.

Taliessin's Return to Logres

The seas were left behind;
in a harbour of Logres
lightly I came to land
under a roaring wind.
Strained were the golden sails,
the masts of the galley creaked
as it rode for the Golden Horn
and I for the hills of Wales.

In a train of golden cars
the Emperor went above,
for over me in my riding
shot seven golden stars,
as if while the great oaks stood,
straining, creaking, around,
seven times the golden sickle
flashed in the Druid wood.

Covered on my back,
untouched, my harp had hung;
its notes sprang to sound
as I took the blindfold track,
the road that runs from tales,
through the darkness where Circe's son
sings to the truants of towns
in a forest of nightingales.

The beast ran in the wood
that had lost the man's mind;
on a path harder than death
spectral shapes stood
propped against trees;
they gazed as I rode by;
fast after me poured
the light of flooding seas.

But I was Druid-sprung;
I cast my heart in the way;
all the Mercy I called
to give courage to my tongue.
As I came by Broceliande
a diagram played in the night,
where either the golden sickle
flashed, or a signalling hand.

Away on the southern seas
was the creaking of the mast;
beyond the Roman road
was the creaking of the trees.
Beyond the farms and the fallows
the sickle of a golden arm
that gathered fate in the forest
in a stretched palm caught the hallows.

At the falling of the first
chaos behind me checked;
at the falling of the second
the wood showed the worst;

at the falling of the third
I had come to the king's camp ;
the harp on my back
syllabled the signal word.

I saw a Druid light
burn through the Druid hills,
as the hooves of King Arthur's horse
rounded me in the night.
I heard the running of flame
faster than fast through Logres
into the camp by the hazels
I Taliessin came.

The Vision of the Empire

α

The organic body sang together;
dialects of the world sprang in Byzantium;
back they rang to sing in Byzantium;
the streets repeat the sound of the Throne.

The Acts issue from the Throne.
Under it, translating the Greek minuscula
to minds of the tribes, the identities of creation
phenomenally abating to kinds and kindreds,
the household inscribes the Acts of the Emperor;
the logothetes run down the porphyry stair
bearing the missives through the area of empire.

Taliessin walked through the hither angels,
from the exposition of grace to the place of images.
The morn brightened on the Golden Horn;
he heard behind him the chariots' clatter
that bore a new matter to all the dialects;
he saw the nuntii loosened on the currents
over the sea, in the mechanism of motion,
rowers' arms jointed to the imperial oars.
Chariots and galleys sprang from the shores;
the messengers were borne over sea and land.
The king's poet gazed in the mirror of the Horn.

6

β

The morn rose on the Golden Horn.
I saw the identities imaged in a sapphire sea :
beyond Sinai Ararat, beyond Ararat Elburz—
light-sprinkling, flaked-snow-sparkling,
chastities of ranged peaks of Caucasus,
snow's glow on the world's brows
changed with deep vales of verdure.
The missives of identity came from the scribes
where the tribes gather and keep holiday
on the name-day and birthday of their father the Emperor.
The Empire's sun shone on each round mound,
double fortalices defending dales of fertility.
The bright blades shone in the craft of the dancing war ;
the stripped maids laughed for joy of the province,
bearing in themselves the shape of the province
founded in the base of space,
in the rounded bottom of the Emperor's glory.
Spines were strengthened, loves settled ;
tossed through aerial gulfs of empire
the lost name, the fool's shame,
fame and frame of lovers in lowlands of Caucasia,
rang round snowy Elburz.
The organic body sang together.

γ

Elburz rose in the Golden Horn.
South from the sea-bone, Thule, the skull-stone,
herbage of lone rock,
the scheme of Logres, the theme of the design of the Empire,

rose in balance and weight, freight of government with
    glory.
Merlin, time's metre, climbs through prisms and lines ;
over near Camelot and far Carbonek,
over the Perilous Sell, the See of union,
the phosphor of Percivale's philosophical star shines.
Lancelot's lion, bewildered by the smell of adoration,
roars round Guinevere's lordly body.
Merlin defines, in blazons of the brain,
shield upon shield, station upon station ;
and the roads resound with the galloping lords.
The swords flash ; the pirates fly ;
the Table stands rigid in the king's hall,
and over their seats the plotted arms of the soul,
which are their feats and the whole history of Logres.
Down the imperial highroad the white nuntius rides
to heighten the hearts of Lateran, Gaul, and Logres.

δ

The milk rises in the breasts of Gaul,
trigonometrical milk of doctrine.
Man sucks it ; his joints harden,
sucking logic, learning, law,
drawing on the breasts of *intelligo* and *credo*.
I, Taliessin, born of the Druids by the sea,
drank also in the schools of Gaul ;
I have drunk at the tables of all the doctors ;
I have modulated song to the waters of Logres,
the running of Thames, the tidal basins.
I heard the iron chariots on the roads of Gaul,

but the fleets took me, distances of the sea ;
the dialect of Logres was an aspect of Byzantium ;
the grand art was taught in the heart of the harbours of Arthur.

ε

The mist rolled down the edge of an old sun ;
mammoth and bear prowled on the broad ledge of the
    shoulders.
Strength articulated itself in morals
of arms, joints, wrists, hands ;
the planes of palms, the mid-points of hid cones,
opened in Lombardy, the cone's point in Rome,
seminal of knowledge, pontifex of the Arval college
of spiralling instincts, all roads (active and passive) from Rome,
to be bridge-builders in Gaul, clerks of audience in Byzantium.
Finger-nails, weaklings of seedtime, scratched the soil
till by iron nails the toil was finished in the time of our need,
the sublime circle of the cone's bottom, the seed-springing
    surrender :
hands of incantation changed to hands of adoration,
the quintuple psalm, the pointing of Lateran :
active and passive in a single mystery,
a single sudden flash of identity,
the heart-breaking manual acts of the Pope.

ζ

Why moves the Pope in the marches of the Empire?
why do the golden palaces pale to the Papal
vesture, flesh and bone of reparation ?
what was the crossing of the will of the Emperor ?

η

The Adam in the hollow of Jerusalem respired :
softly their thought twined to its end,
crying : *O parent, O forkèd friend,*
am I not too long meanly retired
in the poor space of joy's single dimension ?
Does not God vision the principles at war ?
Let us grow to the height of God and the Emperor :
Let us gaze, son of man, on the Acts in contention.

The Adam climbed the tree ; the boughs
rustled, withered, behind them ; they saw
the secluded vision of battle in the law ;
they found the terror in the Emperor's house.

The tree about them died undying,
the good lusted against the good,
the Acts in conflict envenomed the blood,
on the twisted tree hung their body wrying.

Joints cramped ; a double entity
spewed and struggled, good against good ;
they saw the mind of the Emperor as they could,
his imagination of the wars of identity.

He walked slowly through his habitation
in the night of himself without him ; Byzantium slept ;
a white pulsing shape behind him crept,
the ejection to the creature of the creature's rejection of
    salvation.

Conception without control had the Adam of the error ;
stifled over their head, the tree's bright beam
lost in the sides of the pit its aerial stream ;
they had their will ; they saw ; they were torn in the terror.

θ

Elburz sinks through the Golden Horn :
the feet of creation walk backward through the waters.

The single galley hardly moves,
the stiffening mechanic of arms and oars fails ;
patched with undyed canvas the purple sails
drag at the flagging hands of man ;
the sea's unaccumulated distance drags at the sailor's hearts.

The sea-borne Asian mine,
stuff of Caucasia fashioned in Byzantium,
earth's gold sprinkled over the sea
and plated round the poop of the visionary spirit,
shines no longer nor lustily gleams.

On the brazen deck blasts of hot ashes
fall from unseen volcanoes ; harsh birds,
stabbing at sea-broods, grating their mating calls,
cover it ; down their flight gusts drove once the galley.

Phosphorescent on the stagnant level
a headless figure walks in a crimson cope,
volcanic dust blown under the moon.

A brainless form, as of the Emperor,
walks, indecent hands hidden under the cope,
dishallowing in that crimson the flush on the mounds of
    Caucasia.

His guard heaves round him ; heaven-sweeping tentacles
stretch, dragging octopus bodies over the level ;
his cope by two is lifted from his body,
where it walks on the sinking floor of antipodean Byzantium.
Let us gaze, son of man, on the Acts in contention.

Phosphorescent gleams the point of the penis :
rudiments or relics, disappearing, appearing,
live in the forlorn focus of the intellect,
eyes and ears, the turmoil of the mind of sensation.

Inarticulate always on an inarticulate sea
beyond P'o-lu the headless Emperor moves,
the octopuses round him ; lost are the Roman hands ;
lost are the substantial instruments of being.

ι

The organic body sang together ;
the Acts of identity adored their Lord ;
the song sprang and rang in Byzantium.

O you shoulders, elbows, wrists,
bless him, praise him, magnify him for ever ;
you fittings of thumbs and fingers,
bless ye the Lord ;

sockets and balls in knees and ankles,
bless ye the Lord ;
hips, thighs, spine in its multiples,
bless him, praise him, magnify him for ever ;
bless him in Caucasia, bless him in Lateran,
bless him in the blazons of London-in-Logres,
if there be worlds of language beyond Logres,
bless him, praise him, magnify him for ever ;
if there be wit in the rolling mass of waters,
if any regimen in marshes beyond P'o-lu,
if any measurement among the headless places,
bless him, praise him, magnify him for ever.

The Calling of Arthur

Arthur was young ; Merlin met him on the road.
  Wolfish, the wizard stared, coming from the wild,
  black with hair, bleak with hunger, defiled
from a bed in the dung of cattle, inhuman his eyes.

Bold stood Arthur ; the snow beat ; Merlin spoke :
  Now am I Camelot ; now am I to be builded.
  King Cradlemas sits by Thames ; a mask o'ergilded
covers his wrinkled face, all but one eye.

Cold and small he settles his rump in the cushions.
  Through the emerald of Nero one short-sighted eye
  peers at the pedlars of wealth that stand plausibly by.
The bleak mask is gilded with a maiden's motionless smile.

.The high aged voice squeals with callous comfort.
  He sits on the bank of Thames, a sea-snail's shell
  fragile, fragilely carved, cast out by the swell
on to the mud ; his spirit withers and dies.

He withers ; he peers at the tide ; he squeals.
  He warms himself by the fire and eats his food
  through a maiden's motionless mouth ; in his mood
he polishes his emerald, misty with tears for the poor.

The waste of snow covers the waste of thorn ;
  on the waste of hovels snow falls from a dreary sky ;
  mallet and scythe are silent ; the children die.
King Cradlemas fears that the winter is hard for the poor.

Draw now the tide, spring moon, swing now the depth ;
   under the snow that falls over brick and prickle,
   the people ebb ; draw up the hammer and sickle.
The banner of Bors is abroad ; where is the king ?

Bors is up ; his wife Elayne behind him
   mends the farms, gets food from Gaul ; the south
   is up with hammer and sickle, and holds Thames mouth.
Lancelot hastens, coming with wagons and ships.

The sea-snail lies by Thames ; O wave of Pendragon,
   roll it, swallow it ; pull the mask o'ergilded
   from the one-eyed face that blinks at the comfort builded
in London's ruins ; I am Camelot ; Arthur, raise me.

Arthur ran ; the people marched ; in the snow
   King Cradlemas died in his litter ; a screaming few
   fled ; Merlin came ; Camelot grew.
In Logres the king's friend landed, Lancelot of Gaul.

Mount Badon

The king's poet was his captain of horse in the wars.
He rode over the ridge ; his force
sat hidden behind, as the king's mind had bidden.
The plain below held the Dragon in the centre,
Lancelot on the left, on the right Gawaine,
Bors in the rear commanding the small reserve :
the sea's indiscriminate host roared at the City's wall.
As with his household few Taliessin rode over the ridge,
the trumpets blew, the lines engaged.

Staring, motionless, he sat ;
who of the pirates saw ? none stopped ;
they cropped and lopped Logres ; they struck deep,
and their luck held ; only support lacked :
neither for charge nor for ruse could the allied crews
abide the civilized single command ;
each captain led his own band and each captain unbacked ;
but numbers crashed ; Taliessin saw Gawaine
fail, recover, and fail again ;
he saw the Dragon sway ; far away
the household of Lancelot was wholly lost in the fray ;
he saw Bors fling
company after company to the aid of the king,
till the last waited the word alone.

Staring, motionless, he sat.
Dimly behind him he heard how his staff stirred.

One said : " He dreams or makes verse " ; one : " Fool.
all lies in a passion of patience—my lord's rule."
In a passion of patience he waited the expected second.
Suddenly the noise abated, the fight vanished, the last
few belated shouts died in a new quiet.
In the silence of a distance, clear to the king's poet's sight,
Virgil was standing on a trellised path by the sea.
Taliessin saw him negligently leaning ; he felt
the deep breath dragging the depth of all dimension,
as the Roman sought for the word, sought for his thought,
sought for the invention of the City by the phrase.
He saw Virgil's unseeing eyes ; his own,
in that passion of all activity but one suspended,
leaned on those screened ports of blind courage.
Barbaric centuries away, the ghostly battle contended.

Civilized centuries away, the Roman moved.
Taliessin saw the flash of his style
dash at the wax ; he saw the hexameter spring
and the king's sword swing ; he saw, in the long field,
the point where the pirate chaos might suddenly yield,
the place for the law of grace to strike.
He stood in his stirrups ; he stretched his hand ;
he fetched the pen of his spear from its bearer ;
his staff behind signed to their men.

The Æneid's beaked lines swooped on Actium ;
the stooped horse charged ; backward blown,
the flame of song streaked the spread spears
and the strung faces of words on a strong tongue.
The household of Taliessin swung on the battle ;

T.L.   C

hierarchs of freedom, golden candles of the solstice
that flared round the golden-girdled Logos, snowy-haired,
brazen-footed, starry-handed, the thigh banded with the
    Name.

The trumpets of the City blared through the feet of brass ;
the candles flared among the pirates ; their mass broke ;
Bors flung his company forward ; the horse and the reserve
caught the sea's host in a double curve ;
the paps of the day were golden-girdled ;
hair, bleached white by the mere stress of the glory,
drew the battle through the air up threads of light.
The tor of Badon heard the analytical word ;
the grand art mastered the thudding hammer of Thor,
and the heart of our lord Taliessin determined the war.

The lord Taliessin kneeled to the king ;
the candles of new Camelot shone through the fought field.

The Crowning of Arthur

The king stood crowned ; around in the gate,
midnight striking, torches and fires
massing the colour, casting the metal,
furnace of jubilee, through time and town,
Logres heraldically flaunted the king's state.

The lords sheathed their swords ; they camped
by Camelot's wall ; thick-tossed torches,
tall candles flared, opened, deployed ;
between them rose the beasts of the banners ;
flaring over all the king's dragon ramped.

Wars were at end ; the king's friend stood
at the king's side ; Lancelot's lion
had roared in the pattern the king's mind cherished,
in charges completing the strategy of Arthur ;
the king's brain working in Lancelot's blood.

Presaging intelligence of time climbed,
Merlin climbed, through the dome of Stephen,
over chimneys and churches ; from the point of Camelot
he looked through the depth to the dome of Sophia ;
the kingdom and the power and the glory chimed.

He turned where the fires, amid burning mail,
poured, tributaried by torches and candles,
to a point in a massive of colour, one
aureole flame ; the first shield's deep azure,
sidereally pointed, the lord Percivale.

Driving back that azure a sea rose black ;
on a fess of argent rode a red moon.
The Queen Morgause leaned from a casement ;
her forehead's moon swallowed the fires,
it was crimson on the bright-banded sable of Lamorack.

The tincture changed ; ranged the craft
of the king's new champion in a crimson field ;
mockery in mockery, a dolphin naiant ;
a silver fish under bloody waters,
conquered or conquering, Dinadan laughed.

A pelican in golden piety struck well
the triple bloody drops from its wound ;
in strong nurture of instinct, it smote
for its young its breast ; the shield of Bors
bore its rich fervours, to itself most fell.

Shouldering shapes through the skies rise and run,
through town and time ; Merlin beheld
the beasts of Broceliande, the fish of Nimue,
hierarchic, republican, the glory of Logres,
patterns of the Logos in the depth of the sun.

Taliessin in the crowd beheld the compelled brutes,
wildness formalized, images of mathematics,
star and moon, dolphin and pelican,
lion and leopard, changing their measure.
Over the mob's noise rose gushing the sound of the flutes.

Gawaine's thistle, Bedivere's rose, drew near :
flutes infiltrating the light of candles.
Through the magical sound of the fire-strewn air,
spirit, burning to sweetness of body,
exposed in the midst of its bloom the young queen Guinevere.

Lancelot moved to descend ; the king's friend kneeled,
the king's organic motion, the king's mind's blood,
the lion in the blood roaring through the mouth of creation
as the lions roar that stand in the Byzantine glory.
Guinevere's chalice flew red on an argent field.

So, in Lancelot's hand, she came through the glow,
into the king's mind, who stood to look on his city :
the king made for the kingdom, or the kingdom made for the
    king ?
Thwart drove his current against the current of Merlin :
in beleaguered Sophia they sang of the dolorous blow.

Doom in shocks sprinkled the burning gloom,
molten metals and kindling colours pouring
into the pyre ; at the zenith lion and dragon
rose, clawed, twisted, screamed ;
Taliessin beheld a god lie in his tomb.

At the door of the gloom sparks die and revive ;
the spark of Logres fades, glows, fades.
It is the first watch ; the Pope says Matins in Lateran ;
the hollow call is beaten on the board in Sophia ;
the ledge of souls shudders, whether they die or live.

Taliessin's Song of the Unicorn

Shouldering shapes of the skies of Broceliande
  are rumours in the flesh of Caucasia ; they raid the west,
clattering with shining hooves, in myth scanned—
  centaur, gryphon, but lordlier for verse is the crest
of the unicorn, the quick panting unicorn ; he will come
  to a girl's crooked finger or the sharp smell
of her clear flesh—but to her no good ; the strum
  of her blood takes no riot or quiet from the quell ;
she cannot like such a snorting alien love
  galloped from a dusky horizon it has no voice
to explain, nor the silver horn pirouetting above
  her bosom—a ghostly threat but no way to rejoice
in released satiation ; her body without delight
  chill-curdled, and the gruesome horn only to be
polished, its rifling rubbed between breasts ; right
  is the tale that a true man runs and sets the maid free,
and she lies with the gay hunter and his spear flesh-hued,
  and over their couch the spoiled head displayed—
as Lesbia tied horned Catullus—of the cuckold of the
    wood ;
  such, west from Caucasia, is the will of every maid ;
yet if any, having the cunning to call the grand beast,
  the animal which is but a shade till it starts to run,
should dare set palms on the point, twisting from the least
  to feel the sharper impress, for the thrust to stun
her arteries into channels of tears beyond blood
  (O twy-fount, crystal in crimson, of the Word's side),

and she to a background of dark bark, where the wood
  becomes one giant tree, were pinned, and plied
through hands to heart by the horn's longing : O she
  translucent, planted with virtues, lit by throes,
should be called the Mother of the Unicorn's Voice, men see
  her with awe, her son the new sound that goes
surrounding the City's reach, the sound of enskied
  shouldering shapes, and there each science disposed,
horn-sharp, blood-deep, ocean and lightning wide,
  in her paramour's song, by intellectual nuptials unclosed.

Bors to Elayne: The Fish of Broceliande

The king is building Camelot; he has bidden his host
depart to their homes, the wards only of the towns
pricked for weapons; and each lord to his own land.

He has sent me to be his lieutenant on the southern coast,
over ships in the harbours and sheep flocks on the downs;
to define the kingdom—from unpathed Broceliande

to the eastern forelands. In the great hall's glow
Taliessin sang of the sea-rooted western wood;
his song meant all things to all men, and you to me.

A forest of the creatures: was it of you? no?
monstrous beasts in the trees, birds flying the flood,
and I plucked a fish from a stream that flowed to that sea:

from you? for you? shall I drop the fish in your hand?
in your hand's pool? a bright-scaled, red-tailed fish
to dart and drive up the channel of your arm?

the channel of your arm, the piercing entry to a land
where, no matter how lordly at home is set the dish,
no net can catch it, nor hook nor gaff harm?

but it darts up the muscles of the arm, to swim
round the clear boulder of the shoulder, stung with spray,
and down the cataract of the backed spine leaps

into bottomed waters at once clear and dim,
where nets are fingered and flung on many a day ;
yet it slides through the mesh of the mind and sweeps

back to its haunt in a fathomless bottomless pool ;
is there a name then, an anagram of spirit and sense,
that Nimue the mistress of the wood could call it by ?

None but a zany, none but earth's worst fool,
could suppose he knows ; no name was thrown thence ;
some say a twy-nature only can utter the cry

(what ? how?) to bring it from the stirred stream,
and if—inhumanly flashing a sudden scale,
aboriginally shaking the aboriginal main.

Double tracks then their dazzled eyes seem
to follow : one, where the forked dominant tail
flicks, beats, reddens the smooth plane

of the happy flesh ; one, where the Catacomb's stone
holds its diagram over the happy dead
who flashed in living will through the liquid wish.

Will you open your hand now to catch your own
nova creatura ? through stream and cataract sped,
through shallow and depth ? *accipe*, take the fish.

Take ; I have seen the branches of Broceliande.
Though Camelot is built, though the king sit on the throne,
yet the wood in the wild west of the shapes and names

probes everywhere through the frontier of head and hand ;
everywhere the light through the great leaves is blown
on your substantial flesh, and everywhere your glory frames.

Taliessin in the School of the Poets

Through Camelot, which is London-in-Logres,
  by Paul's and Arthur's door,
Taliessin came to the school of the poets;
through an exposition of song,
over a glamour of golden-work,
  his shadow fell on the floor.

Phœbus there in mid-mosaic
  on a mud-born Python trod;
his beams about him enmeshed the world,
London, Rome, and the underseas;
the moving shadow over all
  lapped the edge of the god.

Dusk deepened in the work's width;
  from rituals and prophecies,
from skins of runes and vellums of verse,
the children of song to the brass of a man,
searching the dark of Phœbus' style,
  turned attentive eyes.

Their hearts ached, their thoughts toiled,
  with sorrows and young loves;
within verse they were teased by verse;
Taliessin stood by the chair of the poets;
in the court beyond the lattice
  cooed the king's doves.

27

Butterfly fancies hovered
  round the edged Phœbean shape.
' Fortune befall,' the king's poet said,
' the weighed gold of butterflies' wings,
the measure of the swaying hazel's shade,
  or of light in the neck's nape.

' Skeined be the creamed-with-crimson sphere
  on a guessed and given line,
skeined and swirled on the head-to-heel,
or the radial arms' point-to-point ;
reckoned the rondures of the base
  by the straight absolute spine.

' Swung be the measuring hazel wand
  over thighs and shoulders bare,
and grace-pricked to gules the field
by the intinctured heart's steel ;
but best they fathom the blossom
  who fly the porphyry stair.

' At the huge and heavy stair's head
  all measures, to infinite strength,
from sapphire-laced distances drawn,
fill the jewel-joint-justiced throne ;
adored be God and the Emperor
  for the gathering of the nth.

' From the indulged Byzantine floor
  between right and left newel
floats the magnanimous path of the stair

to a tangle of compensations,
every joint a centre,
   and every centre a jewel.

' Each moment there is the midmost
   of the whole massive load ;
impulse a grace and wonder a will,
love desert, and sight direction,
whence the Acts of Identity issue
   in the Pandects and the Code ;

' while in the opposite shires of Logres
   the willows of the brook sway
by the tribal tracks and the Roman roads
in the haze of the levels and the lengthening lines,
and the nuts of the uncut hazel fall
   down the cut hazel's way.'

Taliessin's voice sharpened
   on Virgil's exact word ;
he uttered Italy seen from a wave ;
he defined the organisms of hell.
Blindfold on their perches
   the king's falcons stirred.

The darkened glamour of the golden-work
   took colour from each line ;
dimly the gazing postulants saw
patterns of multilinear red
sprinkled and spreading everywhere,
   and spaced to one design.

The king's poet stood by the sovereign chair ;
  in a harsh voice he cried
of the stemming and staling of great verse,
of poetry plunged into the void
where Virgil clutched at clumps of song
  when that master of poets died.

Tendebantque manus—there
  in the broad Phœbean ground
they saw the macrocosm drawn ;
they heard the universal sigh
in the balance of changing levels
  and complemented sound.

Infinite patterns opened
  in the sovereign chair's mass ;
but the crowned form of anatomized man,
bones, nerves, sinews,
the diagram of the style of the Logos,
  rose in the crimson brass.

Breathless explorers of the image,
  innocent, lucent-eyed,
the young poets studied precision ;
Taliessin remembered the soul :
Sis salvator, Domine,
  the king's poet sighed.

Taliessin on the Death of Virgil

Virgil fell from the edge of the world,
hurled by the thrust of Augustus' back ; the shape
he loved grew huge and black, loomed and pushed.
The air rushed up ; he fell
into despair, into air's other.
The hexameter's fullness now could find no ground ;
his mind, dizzily replete with the meaningless sweet sound,
could found no Rome there on the joys of a noise.
He fell through his moment's infinity
(no man escapes), all the shapes of his labour,
his infinite images, dropping pell-mell ; above,
loomed the gruesome great buttocks of Augustus his love,
his neighbour, infinitely large, infinitely small.
In the midst of his fall others came, none to save.
While he was dropping they put him in a grave.
Perpetual falling, perpetual burying,
this was the truth of his Charon's ferrying—
everlastingly plucked from and sucked from and plucked to
          and sucked to a grave.

Unborn pieties lived.
Out of the infinity of time to that moment's infinity
they lived, they rushed, they dived below him, they rose
to close with his fall ; all, while man is, that could
live, and would, by his hexameters, found
there the ground of their power, and their power's use.
Others he saved ; himself he could not save.

In that hour they came ; more and faster, they sped
to their dead master ; they sought him to save
from the spectral grave and the endless falling,
who had heard, for their own instruction, the sound of his
    calling.
There was intervention, suspension, the net of their loves,
all their throng's songs :
Virgil, master and friend,
holy poet, priest, president of priests,
prince long since of all our energies' end,
deign to accept adoration, and what salvation
may reign here by us, deign of goodwill to endure,
in this net of obedient loves, doves of your cote and wings,
Virgil, friend, lover, and lord.

Virgil was fathered of his friends.
He lived in their ends.
He was set on the marble of exchange.

The Coming of Palomides

Talaat ibn Kula of Ispahan
taught me the measurement of man
that Euclid and Archimedes showed,
ere I took the Western road
across the strait of the Spanish seas.
Through the green-pennon-skirted Pyrenees,
from the sharp curved line of the Prophet's blade
that cuts the Obedience from the Obeyed,
I came to the cross-littered land of Gaul.
Gospels trigonometrical
measured the height of God-in-man
by the swinging hazels of Lateran
on the hill where Cœlius Vibenna's lamp
twinkled amid the sorcerers' camp
when the Etruscan spells were thrown
over flesh and over bone,
to prevent the City and the See
by the twisted malice of Goetry.
Earth shattered under them, but therethrough
Cæsar rose and the Gospel grew,
till, lit at the star of God-in-man,
burned the candles of Lateran.
But between the magic and the mystery
Julius Cæsar heard of the sea
where trembling fishers are called to row
shadowy-cargoed boats, and know
friction of keels on the soundless coasts.

Julius pierced through the tale of ghosts,
and opened the harbours of the north.
I too from Portius Iccus forth
sailing came to the Logrian land :
there I saw an outstretched hand.

In the summer-house of the Cornish king
I kneeled to Mark at a banqueting,
I saw the hand of the queen Iseult ;
down her arm a ruddy bolt
fired the tinder of my brain
to measure the shape of man again ;
I heard the king say : ' Little we know
of verses here ; let the stranger show
a trick of the Persian music-craft.'
Iseult smiled and Tristram laughed.
Her arm exposed on the board, between
Mark and Tristram sat the queen,
but neither Mark nor Tristram sought
the passion of substantial thought,
neither Mark nor Tristram heard
the accent of the antique word.
Only the uncrossed Saracen
sang amid the heavy Cornish men ;
only, a folly amid fighting lords,
I caught her arm in a mesh of chords,
and the speech of Moslem Ispahan
swung the hazels of Lateran.

Blessed (I sang) the Cornish queen ;
for till to-day no eyes have seen
how curves of golden life define

the straightness of a perfect line,
till the queen's blessed arm became
a rigid bar of golden flame
where well might Archimedes prove
the doctrine of Euclidean love,
and draw his demonstrations right
against the unmathematic night
of ignorance and indolence !
Did, to this new-awakened sense,
he or some greater Master sweep
his compass ? fiery circles leap
round finger-point and shoulder ; arc
with arc encountering strikes a spark
wherefrom the dropping chords of fire
fashion the diagram of desire.
There flames my heart, there flames my thought;
either to double points is caught ;
lo, on the arm's base for a sign,
the single equilateral trine !

Blessed for ever be the hour
when first the intellectual power
saw triple angles, triple sides,
and that proceed which naught divides
through their great centre, by the stress
of the queen's arm's blissful nakedness,
to unions metaphysical ;
blessed the unity of all
authorities of blood and brain,
triply obedient, each to twain,
obedience in the mind, subdued

to fire of fact and fire of blood;
obedience in the blood, exact
to fire of mind and fire of fact;
to mind and blood the fact's intense
incredible obedience,
in the true equilateral ease.

And O what long isosceles
from finger-point and shoulder flies
towards me, and distant strain my eyes
along the twin roads, there to prove
the doctrine of Euclidean love;
let the queen's grace but yield her hand
to be by such strong measure spanned——

In the summer house of the Cornish king
suddenly I ceased to sing.
Down the arm of the queen Iseult
quivered and darkened an angry bolt;
and, as it passed, away and through
and above her hand the sign withdrew.
Fiery, small, and far aloof,
a tangled star in the cedar roof,
it hung; division stretched between
the queen's identity and the queen.
Relation vanished, though beauty stayed;
too long my dangerous eyes delayed
at the shape on the board, but voice was mute;
the queen's arm lay there destitute,
empty of glory; and while the king
tossed the Saracen lord a ring,

and the queen's pleasure, smiling still,
turned to Tristram's plausible skill,
three lines in a golden distance shone,
three points pricked golden and were gone.
Tristram murmured by Iseult's head.

Cœlius Vibenna over the dead
cast the foul Chthonian spells,
on ghost and bone and what lingers else ;
Cæsar heard of the ghostly sea
that masks the ports of the unity ;
the Pope in white, like the ghost of man,
stood in the porch of Lateran ;
and aloof in the roof, beyond the feast,
I heard the squeak of the questing beast,
where it scratched itself in the blank between
the queen's substance and the queen.

Lamorack and the Queen Morgause of Orkney

Hued from the livid everlasting stone
the queen's hewn eyelids bruised my bone ;
my eyes splintered, as our father Adam's when the first
exorbitant flying nature round creation's flank burst.

Her hair was whirlwind about her face ;
her face outstripped her hair ; it rose from a place
where pre-Adamic sculpture on an ocean rock lay,
and the sculpture torn from its rock was swept away.

Her hand discharged catastrophe ; I was thrown
before it ; I saw the source of all stone,
the rigid tornado, the schism and first strife
of primeval rock with itself, Morgause Lot's wife.

I had gone in summer at the king's word to explore
the coast of the kingdom towards the Pole ; the roar
of the ocean beyond all coasts threatened on one hand ;
on the other we saw the cliffs of Orkney stand.

Caves and hollows in the crags were filled with the scream
of seamews nesting and fleeting ; the extreme theme
of Logres rose in harsh cries and hungry storms,
and there, hewn in a cleft, were hideous huge forms.

38

I remembered how the archbishop in Caerleon at a feast
preached that before the making of man or beast
the Emperor knew all carved contingent shapes
in torrid marsh temples or on cold crookt capes.

These were the shapes only the Emperor knew,
unless Cœlius Vibenna and his loathly few,
squat by their pot, by the twisted hazel art
sought the image of that image within their heart.

Sideways in the cleft they lay, and the seamews' wings
everywhere flying, or the mist, or the mere slant of the things
seemed to stir them ; then the edge of the storm's shock
over us obliquely split rock from rock.

Ship and sculpture shuddered ; the crags' scream
mingled with the seamews' ; Logres' convulsed theme
wailed in the whirlwind ; we fled before the storms,
and behind us loosed in the air flew giant inhuman forms.

When from the sea I came again to my stall
King Arthur between two queens sat in a grim hall,
Guinevere on his right, Morgause on his left ;
I saw in her long eyes the humanized shapes of the cleft.

She sat the sister of Arthur, the wife of Lot,
four sons got by him, and one not.
I heard as she stirred the seamews scream again
in the envy of the unborn bastard and the pride of canonical
    Gawaine.

I turned my eyes to the lords ; they sat half-dead.
The young wizard Merlin, standing by me, said :
' Balin had Balan's face, and Morgause her brother's.
Did you not know the blow that darkened each from other's ?

' Balin and Balan fell by mistaken impious hate.
Arthur tossed loves with a woman and split his fate.
Did you not see, by the dolorous blow's might,
the contingent knowledge of the Emperor floating into sight ?

' Over Camelot and Carbonek a whirling creature hovered
as over the Adam in Eden when they found themselves
    uncovered,
when they would know good as evil ; thereon it was showed,
but then they must know God also after that mode.'

The eyes of the queen Morgause were a dark cavern ;
there a crowned man without eyes came to a carved tavern,
a wine-wide cell, an open grave, that stood
between Caerleon and Carbonek, in the skirts of the blind
    wood.

Through the rectangular door the crowned shape went its
    way ;
it lifted light feet : an eyeless woman lay
flat on the rock ; her arm was stretched to embrace
his own stretched arm ; she had his own face.

The shape of a blind woman under the shape of a blind man :
over them, half-formed, the cipher of the Great Ban,
this, below them both, the shape of the blatant beast matched ;
his mouth was open in a yelp ; his feet scratched.

Beyond them a single figure was cut in the rock ;
it was hewn in a gyration of mow and mock ;
it had a weasel's head and claws on hand and feet ;
it twirled under an arch that gave on the city's street.

The child lies unborn in the queen's womb ;
unformed in his brain is the web of all our doom,
as unformed in the minds of all the great lords
lies the image of the split Table and of surreptitious swords.

I am the queen's servant ; while I live
down my eyes the cliff, the carving, the winged things drive,
since the rock, in those fleet lids of rock's hue,
the sculpture, the living sculpture, rose and flew.

Bors to Elayne: on the King's Coins

I came in ; I saw you stand,
in your hand the bread of love, in your head lightness of law.
The uprightness of the multitude stood in your figure ;
my fieldsmen ate and your women served,
while you watched them from the high seat.
When you saw me a southern burst of love
tossed a new smile from your eyes to your mouth,
shaping for that wind's while the corn of your face.
It was said once that your hair was the colour of corn ;
he who said so was capable only to adorn
the margin of parchments drawn in schools of Gaul ;
their doctrine is your hands' main. I am come again
to live from the founts and fields of your hands ;
colour is art, but my heart counts the doctrine.

On the forms of ancient saints, my heroes, your thumbs,
as on a winch the power of man is wound
to the last inch ; there ground is prepared
for the eared and seeded harvest of propinquant goodwill,
drained the reeded marches, cleared the branched jungles
where the unthumbed shapes of apes swung and hung.
Now when the thumbs are muscled with the power of good-
    will
corn comes to the mill and the flour to the house,
bread of love for your women and my men ;
at the turn of the day, and none only to earn ;
in the day of the turn, and none only to pay ;

for the hall is raised to the power of exchange of all
by the small spread organisms of your hands ; O Fair,
there are the altars of Christ, the City extended.
I have ridden all night from organization in London,
ration and rule, and the fault in ration and rule,
law and the flaw in law, to reach to you,
the sole figure of the organic salvation of our good.

The king has set up his mint by Thames.
He has struck coins ; his dragon's loins
germinate a crowded creaturely brood
to scuttle and scurry between towns and towns,
to furnish dishes and flagons with change of food ;
small crowns, small dragons, hurry to the markets
under the king's smile, or flat in houses squat.
The long file of their snouts crosses the empire,
and the other themes acknowledge our king's head.
They carry on their backs little packs of value,
caravans ; but I dreamed the head of a dead king
was carried on all, that they teemed on house-roofs
where men stared and studied them as I your thumbs'
    epigrams,
hearing the City say *Feed my lambs*
to you and the king ; the king can tame dragons to carriers,
but I came through the night, and saw the dragonlets'
    eyes
leer and peer, and the house-roofs under their weight
creak and break ; shadows of great forms
halloed them on, and followed over falling towns.
I saw that this was the true end of our making ;
mother of children, redeem the new law.

They laid the coins before the council.
Kay, the king's steward, wise in economics, said :
'Good ; these cover the years and the miles
and talk one style's dialects to London and Omsk.
Traffic can hold now and treasure be held,
streams are bridged and mountains of ridged space
tunnelled ; gold dances deftly across frontiers.
The poor have choice of purchase, the rich of rents,
and events move now in a smoother control
than the swords of lords or the orisons of nuns.
Money is the medium of exchange.'

Taliessin's look darkened ; his hand shook
while he touched the dragons ; he said 'We had a good
    thought.
Sir, if you made verse you would doubt symbols.
I am afraid of the little loosed dragons.
When the means are autonomous, they are deadly ; when
    words
escape from verse they hurry to rape souls ;
when sensation slips from intellect, expect the tyrant ;
the brood of carriers levels the good they carry.
We have taught our images to be free ; are we glad ?
are we glad to have brought convenient heresy to Logres ? '

The Archbishop answered the lords ;
his words went up through a slope of calm air :
'Might may take symbols and folly make treasure,
and greed bid God, who hides himself for man's pleasure
by occasion, hide himself essentially : this abides—
that the everlasting house the soul discovers

is always another's ; we must lose our own ends ;
we must always live in the habitation of our lovers,
my friend's shelter for me, mine for him.
This is the way of this world in the day of that other's ;
make yourselves friends by means of the riches of iniquity,
for the wealth of the self is the health of the self exchanged.
What saith Heracleitus ?—and what is the City's breath ?—
dying each other's life, living each other's death.
Money is a medium of exchange.'

I have come now to kiss each magnanimous thumb,
muscles of the brain, functions of the City.
I was afraid the Council had turned you into gold,
as was told of Midas who had ass's ears.
What can be saved without order ? and how order ?
Compact is becoming contract ; man only earns, and pays,
the house outside the City burns but the house within is
        enslaved.
What without coinage or with coinage can be saved ?
O lady, your hand held the bread
and Christ the City spread in the extensor muscles of your
        thumbs.

Say—can the law live ?
can the dead king's head live ?
Pray, mother of children, pray for the coins,
pray for Camelot, pray for the king, pray.

The Star of Percivale

By the magical western door in the king's hall
the Lord Percivale harped ; he added no voice ;
between string and string, all accumulated distance of sound,
a star rode by, through the round window, in the sky of
 Camelot.

Taliessin stood in the court ; he played
a borrowed harp ; his voice defined the music.
Languid, the soul of a maid, at service in the hall,
heard, rose, ran fleetly to fall at his feet.

Soft there, quiescent in adoration, it sang :
Lord, art thou he that cometh ? take me for thine.
The music rang ; the king's poet leaned to cry :
See thou do it not ; I too am a man.

The king's poet leaned, catching the outspread hands :
More than the voice is the vision, the kingdom than the king :
the cords of their arms were bands of glory ; the harp
sang her to her feet ; sharply, sweetly, she rose.

The soul of a serving-maid stood by the king's gate,
her face flushed with the mere speed of adoration.
The Archbishop stayed, coming through the morning to the
 Mass,
Hast thou seen so soon, bright lass, the light of Christ's glory ?

She answered : *The light of another, if aught, I bear,*
as he the song of another ; he said : I obey.
And Dubric : *Also thy joy I wear ; shall we fail*
from Percivale's world's orbit, we there once hurled ?

The sun rose, bringing cloud ;
the day-star vanished ; the king's household in the court
waited ; their voices were loud ; they talked of their fights
till the altar centred between lights ; the lords entered.

The nuntius of Byzantium there, the Emperor's logothete,
angelic, white chlamys crimson-girdled, saw in a vision
a new direct earth of sweet joy given
and its fusion with a new heaven, indirect joy of substitution.

The household kneeled ; the Lord Balin the Savage moved
restless, through-thrust with a causeless vigil of anger ;
the king in the elevation beheld and loved himself crowned ;
Lancelot's gaze at the Host found only a ghost of the Queen.

The Ascent of the Spear

Taliessin walked in the palace yard;
he saw, under a guard, a girl sit in the stocks.
The stable-slaves, lounging by the gate,
cried catcalls and mocks, flung roots and skins of fruits.
She, rigid on the hard bench, disdained
motion, her cheek stained with a bruise, veined
with fury her forehead. The guard laughed and chaffed;
when Taliessin stepped near, he leapt to a rigid salute.
Lightly the king's poet halted, took the spear
from the manned hand, and with easy eyes dismissed.
Nor wist the crowd, he gone, what to do;
lifted arms fell askew; jaws gaped;
claws of fingers uncurled. They gazed,
amazed at the world of each inflexible head.

The silence loosened to speech; the king's poet said:
'Do I come as a fool? forgive folly; once more
be kind, be faithful: did we not together adore?
Say then what trick of temper or fate?' Hard-voiced,
she said without glancing, 'I sit here for taking a stick
to a sneering bastard slut, a Mongol ape,
that mouthed me in a wrangle.
Fortunate, for a brawl in the hall, to escape,
they dare tell me, the post, the stripping and whipping:
should I care, if the hazel rods cut flesh from bone?'
'Ah lady,' the king's poet murmured, 'confess yes,
except in the stress of a sin worse than the rage.

Though the High Steward's needful law punish the flaw,
wrong not us with pride of guilt or no guilt.
Be witness, Virgil, I too have been rash
to curse the praters and graters of verse.
Engage the flash of thy pardon, Omnipotence, there !
But here before this crowd,
do we amiss ? are we proud ? ' Burning red,
with the laugh half-sob, she said :
' We do amiss—if we—— ' : and he :
' You whose arrogant hands would not cast one skin,
beloved, will you be wroth with your own poor kin ?
Though the Caucasian theme throb with its dull ache
make, lady, the Roman motion ; undo
the fierce grasp from the bench ; lay on the spear-shaft ;
climb gently ; clasp
the massive of light, in whose point serene and severe
Venus, Percivale's planet, phosphor and hesper, is here.'
She obeyed ; she made assent and ascent :
she laid below his her hand on the shaft :
under the Direction she denied pride ;
her heart flowed to the crowd.

By Taliessin's side a demure chamberlain spoke :
' The High Steward to the king's poet : the lord Kay to the
      lord Taliessin :
if who sits here be his friend,
her fetter is his to keep or end.'
' Nor mine,' the king's poet said, ' to prefer. Sir,
she is, of force, at hand : ask her,
and do, either way, a grace of thanks to my lord.'
The messenger glanced. Celestialling the word,

her colour a deference still,
her voice adored and implored : 'Lord, what choice?'
  Who :
'True ; yet if the king's servant and yours could speak,
he might hold it for heaven's best skill
to treat the world's will but as and at the world's will.'
'They will say——' she began ; and he :
'—either way ; they will use to call either side
pride (to stay) or fear (to go).
Do they—do we—know ?   Love, and do what you choose.'
She said : 'I will take the Steward's grace :
do I well ?' 'Is it I then,' the king's poet said, 'whose face
Christ beholds now suffused and sufficed with his brilliant
  blood ?
whom the feline guile of Omnipotence lures ?'
The chamberlain with a sly smile offered the keys.
Taliessin signed them away.   'Release ?
Let come the fellow whose duty unlocks the stocks' bar :
is it ours to undo
the fetter whereto the world's order consigned
its own disordered mind ?'

Aching, stiff, she rose, stumbled, fell ;
the king's poet caught her.   'So are the guilty taught,
sweet friend, who sit in the pass of the Perilous Sell.'
She said, 'I was wrong from beginning——' 'Not to an end.
O new Pheilippides, that stumble was Marathon won.
Remains but the triumph's race to run.'

The Sister of Percivale

The horizon of sensation ran north at the back of Gaul;
Taliessin lay on the wall; a bright fork
from the sky of July flicked hall and horizon.

He lay between both in a morn's mist of making;
idleness cured sloth; his voice
rove and drove words to the troth of ambiguous verse.

In the yard below him a slave's back bent to a well;
it was scarred from whip or sword; the mark
flickered white in the light; hard she swung the handle.

The scar lightened over a curved horizon,
a flash, even in daylight, beheld by heightened eyes,
over the back, a track brightened by boundary peaks.

Jura, Alp, Elburz, Gaul to Caucasia,
eastward; the hall westward cut the sky;
beyond it Percivale's duchy, Wales, and all Broceliande.

She swung from the hips; the handle hard-creaking
cut the voice of Lancelot speaking to the nuntius.
The horizon in her eyes was breaking with distant Byzantium.

Taliessin saw the curved bottom of the world;
his heart—swollen with wonder—swerved on the smooth
    slopes,
reserved always the ride through the themes and Hesper for
    guide.

A round plane of water rose shining in the sun ;
she steadied the handle, the strain ceased ; her arm
balanced the line of the spine and reached for the gain.

Taliessin, watching, played with a line : ' O
Logres centre, can we know what proportion
bear the radii so to the full circumference everywhere ? '

A trumpet's sound from the gate leapt level with the arm,
round with breath as that with flesh, to a plan
blown as that bone-patterned, bound each to a point.

The sound sprang aloft from the western gate ;
a new fate had ridden from the hidden horizon ;
its luck struck as her shoulders took the weight of the water.

In her other outflung arm the sound doubled ; she cast
one look at herself in the drawn flood and passed ;
blent as she went with the blast was the voice of Percivale.

As she at her image Taliessin at the double grace
gazed in the yard ; hemispheres altered place ;
there first and then he saw the rare face of Blanchefleur.

She stood between her brothers, the lords Percivale and
    Lamorack ;
horizon had no lack of horizon ; the circle closed ;
the face of Blanchefleur was the grace of the Back in the Mount.

Her gown was marked with a curve of gold on each breast ;
from a golden brooch the mid-gold ran down to the hem ;
the red track of the back was shown in a front of glory.

Percivale saw his verse-brother lying alone,
rapt on the just glory of the sacred Throne,
the lore of the Emperor patterned in the blast and bone.

Percivale called, saying : ' Sir, speak ;
or is the king's poet weak from Caucasian journeys ?
does the stress of the Empire tire the study of Greek
    minuscula ? '

Taliessin leapt from the wall to greet the princess,
saying : ' Bless me, transit of Venus ! '
The stress of the scar ran level with the star of Percivale.

' Scars and lightnings are the edge of the spun wheel ;
spun is the reel to the height ; the plane revolves ;
the peal breaks from the bone and the way of union speaks.

' Blessed is the eyed axis of both horizons,
and the wheel that taxes the hips and generates the sphere,
and illumination that waxes in the full revolution.'

Proportion of circle to diameter, and the near asymptote
Blanchefleur's smile ; there in the throat her greeting
sprang, and sang in one note the infinite decimal.

The Son of Lancelot

The Lupercalia danced on the Palatine
among women thrusting under the thong; vicars
of Rhea Silvia, vestal, Æneid, Mars-seeded,
mother of Rome; they exulted in the wolf-month.
The Pope's eyes were glazed with terror of the Mass;
his voice shook on Lateran, saying the Confiteor.
Over Europe and beyond Camelot the wolves ranged.

Rods of divination between Lupercal and Lateran :
at the height of the thin night air of Quinquagesima,
in Camelot, in the chamber of union, Merlin dissolved
the window of horny sight on a magical ingress ;
with the hazel of ceremony, fetched to his hand—cut,
smoothed, balsamed with spells, blessed with incision—
he struck from the body of air the anatomical
body of light; he illustrated the high grades.
In the first circle he saw Logres and Europe
sprinkled by the red glow of brute famine
in the packed eyes of forest-emerging wolves,
heaped fires in villages, torches in towns,
lit for safety ; flat, frozen, trapped
under desecrated parallels, clawed perceptions
denounced to a net of burning plunging eyes,
earth lay, at the knots the protective fires ;
and he there, in his own point of Camelot,
of squat snow houses and huddled guards.

Along the print of the straight and sacred hazel
he sent his seeing into the second sphere :
to the images of accumulated distance, tidal figures
shaped at the variable climax of temperatures ; the king
dreaming of a red Grail in an ivory Logres
set for wonder, and himself Byzantium's rival
for men's thuribled and throated worship—magic
throws no truck with dreams ; the rod thrust by :
Taliessin beneath the candles reading from Bors
letters how the Moslem hunt in the Narrow Seas
altogether harried God and the soul out of flesh,
and plotting against the stresses of sea and air
the building of a fleet, and the burning blazon-royal
flying on a white field in the night—the hazel
drove, slowly humming, through spirals of speculation,
and Merlin saw, on the circle's yonder edge,
Blanchefleur, Percivale's sister, professed at Almesbury
to the nuns of infinite adoration, veiled
passions, sororal intellects, earth's lambs,
wolves of the heavens, heat's pallor's secret
within and beyond cold's pallor, fires
lit at Almesbury, at Verulam, at Canterbury, at Lateran,
and she the porter, she the contact of exchange.

Merlin grew rigid ; down the implacable hazel
(a scar on a slave, a verse in Virgil, the reach
of an arm to a sickle, love's means to love)
he sent his hearing into the third sphere—
once by a northern poet beyond Snowdon
seen at the rising of the moon, the *mens sensitiva*,

the feeling intellect, the prime and vital principle,
the pattern in heaven of Nimue, time's mother on earth,
Broceliande. Convection's tides cease
there, temperature is steady to all tenderness
in the last reach of the hazel; fixed is the full.
He knew distinction in three abstractions of sound,
the women's cry under the thong of Lupercal,
the Pope's voice singing the Glory on Lateran,
the howl of a wolf in the coast of Broceliande.
The notes of Lupercal and Lateran ceased; fast
Merlin followed his hearing down the wolf's howl
back into sight's tritosphere—thence was Carbonek
prodigiously besieged by a feral famine; a single
wolf, grey and gaunt, that had been Lancelot,
imbruted, watching the dark unwardened arch,
crouched on the frozen snow beyond Broceliande.

Pelles the Wounded King lay in Carbonek,
bound by the grating pain of the dolorous blow;
his flesh from dawn-star to noontide day by day
ran as a woman's under the moon; in midsun
he called on the reckless heart of God and the Emperor;
he commended to them and commanded himself and his
    land.
Now in the wolf-month nine moons had waned
since Lancelot, ridden on a merciful errand, came
that night to the house; there, drugged and blurred
by the medicated drink of Brisen, Merlin's sister,
he lay with the princess Helayne, supposed Guinevere.
In the morning he saw; he sprang from the tall window;

he ran into a delirium of lycanthropy ; he grew
backward all summer, laired in the heavy wood.
In autumn King Pelles' servants brought him news
of a shape glimpsed on the edge of Broceliande,
a fear in the forest, a foe by the women's well.

Patient, the king constrained patience, and bade
wait till the destined mother's pregnancy was done.
All the winter the wolf haunted the environs of Carbonek ;
now what was left of the man's contrarious mind
was twinned and twined with the beast's bent to feed ;
now it crept to swallow the seed
of love's ambiguity, love's taunt and truth.
Man, he hated ; beast, he hungered ; both
stretched his sabres and strained his throat ; rumble
of memories of love in the gaunt belly told
his instinct only that something edible might come.
Slavering he crouched by the dark arch of Carbonek,
head-high howling, lusting for food, living
for flesh, a child's flesh, his son's flesh.

And infinite beyond him the whole Empire contracted
from (within it) wolves, and (without it) Moslems.
The themes fell back round separate defensive fires ;
there only warmth dilated ; there they circled.
Caucasia was lost, Gaul was ravaged, Jerusalem
threatened ; the crescent cut the Narrow Seas,
while from Cordovan pulpits the iconoclastic
heretical licentiates of Manes denounced union,
and only Lupercal and Lateran preserved Byzantium.

Helayne, Lancelot's bed-fellow, felt her labour.
Brisen knelt; Merlin watched her hands;
the children of Nimue timed and spaced the birth.
Contraction and dilation seized the substance of joy,
the body of the princess, but in her stayed from terror,
from surplus of pain, from outrage, from the wolf in
    flesh,
such as racked in a cave the Mother of Lupercal
and now everywhere the dilating and contracting Empire.
The child slid into space, into Brisen's hands.
Polished brown as hazel-nuts his eyes
opened on his foster-mother; he smiled at space.
Merlin from the hazel's divination saw
the child lie in his sister's hands; he saw
over the Empire the lucid flash of all flesh,
shining white on the sullen white of the snow.
He ran down the hazel; he closed the window; he
    came
past the royal doors of dream, where Arthur, pleased
with the Grail cooped for gustation and God for his glory,
the æsthetic climax of Logres, softly slept;
but the queen's tormented unæsthetic womanhood
alternately wept and woke, her sobs crushed
deep as the winter howls were high, her limbs
swathed by tentacles, her breasts sea-weighed.
Across the flat sea she saw Lancelot
walking, a grotesque back, the opposite of a face
looking backward like a face; she burst the swollen sea
shrieking his name; nor he turned nor looked,
but small on the level dwindled to a distant manikin,
the tinier the more terrible, the sole change

in her everlastingness, except, as Merlin passed,
once as time passed, the hoary waters
laughed backward in her mouth and drowned her tongue.

Through London-in-Logres Merlin came to the wall,
the soldiers saw him; their spears clapped.
For a blade's flash he smiled and blessed their guard,
and went through the gate, beyond the stars' spikes—
as beyond palisades to everywhere the plunging fires,
as from the *mens sensitiva*, the immortal tenderness,
magically exhibited in the ceremonial arts,
to the raging eyes, the rearing bodies, the red
carnivorous violation of intellectual love,
and the frozen earth whereon they ran and starved.
Far as Lancelot's dwindling back from the dumb
queen in a nightmare of the flat fleering ocean,
the soldiers saw him stand, and heard as if near—
far to sight, near to sound—the small
whistling breath in the thin air of Quinquagesima
of the incantation, the manner of the second working.
Then the tall form on the frozen snow
dilated to monstrosity, swelling as if power
entered it visibly, from all points of the wide
sky of the wolf-month : the shape lurched and fell,
dropping on all fours, lurched and leapt and ran,
a loping terror, hurtling over the snow,
a giant white wolf, diminishing with distance,
till only to their aching eyes a white atom
spiralled wildly on the white earth, and at last
was lost; there the dark horizontal edge
of a forest closed their bleak world.

Between the copses on the coast of Broceliande
galloped the great beast, the fierce figure
of universal consumption, Lupercal and Lateran,
taunt of truth, love's means to love
in the wolf-hour, as to each man in each man's hour
the gratuitous grace of greed, grief, or gain,
the measure pressed and overrunning ; now the cries
were silent on Lupercal, the Pope secret on Lateran.
Brisen in Helayne's chamber heard the howl
of Lancelot, and beyond it the longer howl of the air
that gave itself up in Merlin ; she felt him come.
She rose, holding the child ; the wolf and the other,
the wind of the magical wintry beast, broke
together on her ears ; the child's mouth opened ;
his wail was a song and a sound in the third heaven.
Down the stair of Carbonek she came to the arch
and paused beneath ; the wolf's hair rose on his hackles.
He dragged his body nearer ; he was hungry for his son.

The Emperor in Byzantium nodded to the exarchs ;
it was night still when the army began to move,
embarking, disembarking, before dawn Asia
awoke to hear the songs, the shouts, the wheels
of the furnished lorries rolling on the roads to the east,
and the foremost outposts of mountaineers scanning
the mouths of the caves in snowy Elburz, where hid
the hungry Christian refugees, their land
wholly abandoned to beast and Manichæan :
the city on the march to renew the allegiance of
    Caucasia.

A white wolf drove down the wood's path,
flying on the tender knowledge of the third heaven
out into moonlight and Brisen's grey eyes.
She called : ' Be blessed, brother ' ; the child sang :
' blessed brother,' and nestled to its first sleep.
Merlin broke from the wood and crouched to the leap ;
the father of Galahad smelt his coming ; he turned,
swerving from his hunger to the new danger, and
    sprang.
The driving shoulder of Merlin struck him in mid-air
and full the force of the worlds flung ; helpless
he was twisted and tossed in vacancy ; nine yards off
the falling head of Lancelot struck the ground.
Senseless he lay ; lined in the lupine shape,
dimly, half-man, half-beast, was Lancelot's form.
Brisen ran ; with wrappings of crimson wool
she bound the child to her crouching brother's back ;
kissed them both, and dismissed ; small and asleep,
and warm on a wolf's back, the High Prince rode into
    Logres.

Blanchefleur sat at Almesbury gate ; the sleeping
sisters preserved a dreamless adoration.
Blanchefleur prayed for Percivale and Taliessin,
lords in her heart, brothers in the grand art,
exchanging tokens ; for the king and queen ; for Lancelot
nine months lost to Logres ; for the house-slaves
along whose sinewy sides the wolf-cubs leapt,
played in their hands, laired in their eyes, romped
in the wrestle of arms and thighs, cubs of convection,

haggard but held in the leash, foster-children
of the City, foster-fellows of the Merciful Child.
Suddenly, as far off as Blanchefleur deep
in exchange with the world, love's means to love,
she saw on the clear horizon an atom, moving,
waxing, white in white, speed in snow,
a silver shape in the moonlight changing to crimson,
a line of launched glory.

                      The child of Nimue
came, carrying the child of grace in flesh,
truth and taunt inward and outward ; fast
Merlin ran through Logres in the wolf-month
before spring and the leaf-buds in the hazel-twigs.
Percivale's sister rose to her feet ; her key
turned, and Almesbury gate opened ; she called :
' Sister,' but the white wolf lay before her ; alone
she loosened the crimson wrappings from the sleeping
    Galahad ;
high to her breast she held the child ; the wolf
fled, moving white upon motionless white,
the marks of his paws dark on the loosening snow,
and straight as the cross-stamped hazel in the king's house.
The bright intellects of passion gathered at the gate
to see the veiled blood in the child's tender cheeks ;
glowing as the speed in the face of the young Magian
when at dawn, laughing, he came to London-in-Logres ;
or the fire built in Carbonek's guest-chamber
where Lancelot lay tended, housed and a man,
to be by Easter healed and horsed for Logres ;

where at Easter the king's whole household
in the slanting Latin of the launched legions sang
Gaudium multum annunciamus ;
nunc in saecula servi amamus ;
civitas dulcis aedificatur ;
quia qui amat Amor amatur.

Palomides Before his Christening

When I came out of the cave the sky had turned.
I have climbed since down a dead mountain,
over fossils of space in the petrifaction of time,
by the track at the slant-eyes' edge to the city of astrologers.

Astrologers and astronomers alike would starve here;
the rocks are too hard to give any roots room.
No earth-shock alters the infinite smooth formation,
nor anywhere in the monstrous markings are lifting latches.

I determined, after I saw Iseult's arm,
to be someone, to trap the questing beast
that slid into Logres out of Broceliande
through the blank between the queen's meaning and the queen.

Having that honour I would consent to be christened,
I would come then to the Table on my own terms,
bringing a capture by which Christendom might profit,
which Pelles the wounded master could not recover.

But things went wrong; Tristram knocked me sprawling
under the tender smile of Iseult; my manhood,
chivalry, and scimitar-play learned from the Prophet,
could not gain me the accurate flash of her eyes.

Once I overthrew Lancelot by cheating at a tourney,
whence, enraged, fleeing, I was taken by pirates;
Lancelot freed me—he rode on to Carbonek;
Did I smile when I heard that he my saviour was mad?

For bees buzzed down Iseult's arm in my brain ;
black gnats, whirring mosquitoes ; the cream
everywhere dissolved into a spinning cloud ;
and I thought if I caught the beast they would cease certainly.

They would vanish ; the crowd's mass of open mouths,
the City opening its mouth, would certainly swallow them.
There would be nothing but to admire the man
who had done what neither Tristram nor Lancelot did.

In the blank between the queen's meaning and the queen
first I followed my self away from the city
up a steep trail. Dinadan rode past me,
calling : ' Friend, the missing is often the catching.'

But I climbed ; I bruised my ankles on gaunt shapes,
knees, wrists, thighs ; I climbed up a back ;
my feet jarred on the repetition of shoulders ;
crevasses showed their polished slippery sides.

At other times I clambered over house-roofs,
without doors ; on their blank sides
the king's knights were flat cracks, chinks,
rubbed patches, their heads grey blobs.

At last, above them all, I came to a cave,
and a heap of twigs some traveller had left ;
I rubbed a fire and sat within ; the beast
lay at the cave's mouth ; I was glad of its company.

The fire burned awhile ; now I know
time was petrifying without. I sat and scratched.
Smoke in a greasy thickness rolled round the cave,
from flames of fierce fancy, flesh-fire-coloured.

Fire of the flesh subsided to ache of the bone ;
the smoke rolled out, faded, died ;
the beast, as the smoke thinned, had disappeared ;
starveling, I lay in bone on the cave's floor.

Bone lay loving bone it imagined near it,
bone of its hardness of longing, bone of its bone,
skeleton dreaming of skeleton where there was none.
From the cave the greasy smoke drifted slowly outward.

Skeleton dreamed of skeleton it loved to neighbour,
thigh yearning for thigh, humerus for humerus ;
by infinitesimal jerks on the cave's floor
it thrust sideways to the shining cates it imagined.

Bones grew brittle ; sinews yielded ; spirit
hated the air, the moving current that entered,
movements in the cubical plot of the cave, when smoke
emptied, and bones broke ; it was dull day.

Spirit spread in the cave, hating the air.
Bat-like, it hung to the roughness of rock ; it lay
sucking the hollow cavities, less than a bat,
in bones where once it had found a nourishing marrow.

At last the bats frightened me ; I left
my pretties ; airy currents blew my light
flimsy ash to the cave's mouth.   There
was the track ; it went over the mountain to Caerleon.

The sky had turned round ; I could not think
why I should not be christened in the city of astrologers.
It was true I should look a fool before everyone ;
why not look a fool before everyone ?

The Chi-Ro is only a scratching like other scratchings ;
but in the turn of the sky the only scratching—
in a world of rock and one thing other than rock,
the small, slender, pointed, crimson beast ;

the scratching, biting, sliding, slithering thing,
whisking about in unreachable crevasses and cracks,
in cliffs and boulders ;   the smooth-backed head-cocked
snout, and fat rump, and claws on the rock ;

the blatant agile beast.   The lord Dinadan
laughed for joy when once I triumphed in the tourney ;
he called to the lords : ' This is his day ' ; to me :
' Catch as catch can ; but absence is a catch of the presence.

' Sir, if ever in a blank between this and that,
the sky turns on you, and the path slides
to the edge not the front of the eyes, come and be christened.
I will stand your godfather at the pool in Caerleon.'

Dull, undimensioned, I ride at last to Dinadan ;
he is the only lord without a lady ;
he fights and is not enclosed in fight ; he laughs
but he has not the honour and the irony of the court of culture.

The Coming of Galahad

In the hall all had what food they chose;
they rose then, the king, Lancelot, the queen;
they led the young man Galahad to Arthur's bed.
The bishops and peers, going with the royalties, made
ceremony; they created a Rite. When he was laid,
and the order done, the lords went to their rooms.
The queen all night lay thinking of Lancelot's son.

At their rising the king's poet alone had gone
another way; he took the canals of the palace,
the lower corridors, between maids and squires,
past the offices and fires of the king's kitchens,
till he came by a door cleft in a smooth wall
into the outer yards, the skied hall of the guards,
grooms, and scullions. He looked above; he saw
through the unshuttered openings of stairs and rooms
the red flares of processional torches and candles
winding to the king's bed; where instead
of Arthur Galahad that night should lie,
Helayne's son instead of the king's, Lancelot's
instead of Guinevere's, all taken at their word,
their professions, their oaths; the third heaven heard
their declarations of love, and measured them the medium
    of exchange.

He stood looking up among the jakes and latrines;
he touched his harp, low-chanting a nursery rhyme:

'Down the porphyry stair the queen's child ran;
there he played with his father's crown . . .'
A youth came up in the dark, the king's scavenger,
large-boned, fresh-coloured, flame-haired,
Gareth, a prince and a menial, the son of Morgause,
sent from Orkney and the skull-stone in the sea,
to be for cause of obedience set to the worst work.
None at Caerleon knew him but his brother Gawaine
and the king's poet who saw the profile of his mother,
in a grace of fate and a face too soon to be dead.
Hearing him now, Taliessin half-turned his head,
saying : ' Sir ? ' Gareth said, looking at the light :
' Lord, tell me of the new knight.'

Taliessin answered, sounding the strings still :
' Is it not known he is strange, being nurtured till,
men say, but yesterday, among the White Nuns,
by the sister of Percivale, the '—his harp sang—' princess
    Blanchefleur ? '

Gareth said : ' Lord, bless me with more.
Among the slaves I saw from the hall's door
over the meal a mystery sitting in the air—
a cup with a covered fitting under a saffron veil,
as of the Grail itself : what man
is this for whom the Emperor lifts the Great Ban ? '

Taliessin stayed the music ; he said :
' My lords and fathers the Druids between the hazels
touched poems in chords ; they made tell
of everywhere a double dance of a stone and a shell,
and the glittering sterile smile of the sea that pursues.'

Gareth answered : 'I heard it read from a book
by a Northern poet, and once I seemed to look
on Logres pouring like ocean after a girl
who ran in the van, and her hands before her stretched
shone—bright shell, transparent stone,
and the sea touched her, and suddenly by a wind was blown
back, and she mounted a wind and rode away,
and measurement went with her and all sound,
and I found myself weeping there like a fool.'

                                          ' To-day
the stone was fitted to the shell,' the king's poet said ;
' when my lord Sir Lancelot's son sat in the perilous sell,
if he be Sir Lancelot's ; in Logres the thing is done,
the thing I saw wherever I have gone—
in five houses, and each house double : the boughs
of the Druid oak, the cover of gay strokes in the play
of Caucasia, the parchments of Gaul, the altar-stone
in Lateran or Canterbury, the tall Byzantine hall—
O the double newels at the ground of the porphyry stair !
O there the double categories of shell and stone,
and the Acts of Identity uttered out of the Throne.'

' And I among dung and urine—am I one
with shell or stone,' Gareth asked, ' in the jakes ? '
But Taliessin : ' And what makes the City ? to-morrow
you shall be a prince of Orkney again ; to-night
abandon the degrees of Gawaine your brother ; consent
to be nothing but the shape in the gate of excrement,
while Galahad in peace and the king's protection sleeps :
question and digestion, rejection and election,
winged shapes of the Grail's officers, double

grand equality of the State, common of all lives,
common of all experience, sense and more ;
adore and repent, reject and elect. Sir,
without this alley-way how can man prefer ?
and without preference can the Grail's grace be stored ? '

A girl said suddenly beside them : ' Lord,
tell me the food you preferred——' ; and he : ' More
choice is within the working than goes before.
The good that was there—and did I well then ? yes ? '
She said : ' Yes ; yet has all food one taste ?
felicity does not alter ? ' He answered in haste :
' Felicity alters from its centre ; but I—free
to taste each alteration, and that within reach
then and there ; why change till the range twirls ? ' The girl's
eyes turned to the black palace and back.
She said : ' This morning when the Saracen prince was
        christened
dimly the lord Percivale's pentagram glistened
in the rain-dark stones of his eyes : what food there ? '

Taliessin answered : ' Five cells the world
gave me, five shells of multiple sound ;
but when I searched for the paths that joined the signs,
lines of the pentagram's frame, the houses fled
instead to undimensioned points   their content slid
through the gate of the winged prince of the jakes ; pale
they fluttered in an empty fate ; the Child lay dead
in his own gate of growth—and what then,
lady, for you or me or the Saracen,
when the cut hazel has nothing to measure ? ' ' I have known,'

she said, with the scintillation of a grave smile,
' the hazel's stripes on my shoulders ; the blessed luck
of Logres has a sharp style, since I was caught free
from the pirate chaos savaging land and sea ;
is the shell thus also hidden in the stone ? '
' Also thus,' he said, ' if the heart fare
on what lies ever now on the board, stored
meats of love, laughter, intelligence, and prayer.
Is it thus?' and she : 'Who knows?—and who does not care?—
yet my heart's cheer may hope, if Messias please.
Is this the colour of my lord Galahad's eyes ? '

He said : ' The eyes of my lord are the measure of intensity
and his arms of action ; the hazel, Blanchefleur, he.
The clerks of the Emperor's house study the redaction
of categories into identity : so we.
Give me your hand.' Lightly she obeyed, and he
as lightly kissed : ' O office of all lights
from the king's scavenger to the king's substitute, mean
of the merciful Child, common of all rites,
winged wonder of shell and stone, here
a shoot of your own third heaven takes root in Logres.'

Gareth said : ' Lord, before the meal,
when he washed his hands, the water became phosphorescent ;
did you not see ? ' and he : ' Sanctity
common and crescent ! I have seen it flushed anew
in each motion and mode of the princess Blanchefleur ;
who walked dropping light, as all our beloved do.
It is the shell of adoration and the grand art.
But I looked rather to-night at the queen's hand

lying on her heart, and the way her eyes scanned
the unknown lord who sat in the perilous sell.
The bone of the fingers showed through the flesh ; they
    were claws
wherewith the queen's grace gripped : this was the stone
fitting itself to its echo.'

                    He turned to the gate
into the outer air ; she let cry :
' Lord, make us die as you would have us die.'

But he : ' Proofs were ; roofs were : I
what more ? creeds were ; songs were. Four
zones divide the empire from the Throne's firmament,
slanted to each cleft in each wall, with planets planted :
Mercury, thinning and thickening, thirsting to theft ;
Venus preference—though of the greatest, preference ;
O Earth between, O seen and strewn by the four !
Jupiter with a moon of irony and of defeated irony,
and Saturn circled, girdled by turned space.
The moon of irony shone on Lancelot at Carbonek,
the moon of defeated irony on Blanchefleur at Almesbury ;
her hands and head were the shell bursting from the stone
after it has bred in the stone ; she was bright with the moon's
    light
when truth sped from the taunt ; well she nurtured Galahad.
Logres is come into Jupiter ; all the zones
circle Saturn, spinning against the glory,
all the Throne's points, themes of the Empire.'

Emeralds of fire, blank to both, his eyes
were points of the Throne's foot that sank through Logres.

The Departure of Merlin

The Pope stands at Lateran's stone ; man's
heart throbs from his vicarious hands.
The themes are pointed with a new device of brightness,
Trebizond with sun, Archangel with ice.

The blessing of Byzantium befriends the world's ends ;
the great heretical doctors, Moslem and Manichæan,
fly ; in time-spanned Camelot the Table changes ;
the method of phenomena is indrawn to Broceliande.

Merlin bore Lancelot's child to a moon of white nuns,
a knot of nurture in a convent of spirits and suns ;
thence in the perilous throne is the Child's moon risen,
pillars of palace and prison changed to the web of a wood.

The joyous moon waxes in the chair ;
the blessed young sorcerer, a boy and less than a boy,
rose and ran, turning on the roads ; he span
into the heart's simultaneity of repose.

Joseph of Nazareth, Joseph of Arimathea,
came dancing through the coeval-rooted world's idea.
They saw Merlin descending : they met him in the wood,
foster-fathers of beatitude to the foster-father of Galahad ;

twin suns of womb and tomb ; there no strife
is except growth from the roots, nor reaction but repose ;
vigours of joy drive up ; rich-ringed moments
thick in their trunks thrive, young-leaved their voices.

Moons and suns that rose in rites and runes
are come away from sequence, from rules of magic ;
here all is cause and all effect ; the laws
of Merlin's boyhood are unknown in Nimue's wood.

I saw from the deck of a galley becalmed in the seas
Merlin among the trees ; the headless form faded ;
throngs of trunks covered the volcanic waters ;
only the flat djongs float into alien P'o-Lu.

The sailors stared at the thick wood ; one,
ghastly and gaping, despaired of joy ; he yelled
for horror and leapt from the deck to the phosphorescence,
to the wreck of wisdom, the drowned last of love.

The purple sail moved in the wind of Broceliande ;
the sailors sprang to the oars ; the sea-call sang
bidding tack—near and far infinite and equal—
on the visionary ocean track to the port of Byzantium.

More than the fable of Dryads is troth to the Table
in the growth of hazel and elm, oak and bamboo ;
voice of all moments covers who hears as he goes
rich-ringed, young-leaved, monstrous trunks rejoice.

Time's president and precedent, grace ungrieved,
floating through gold-leaved lime or banked behind beech
to opaque green, through each membraned and tissued ex-
    perience
smites in simultaneity to times variously veined.

She who is Nimue, lady of lakes and seas,
articulation of limbs, accumulation of distance,
brings all natural becoming to her shape of immortal being,
as to a flash of seeing the women in the world's base.

Well has Merlin spoken the last spell,
worked the last image, gone to his own :
the moon waxes and wanes in the perilous chair,
where time's foster-child sits, Lancelot's son.

The Death of Palomides

Air strives with wings, wings with air.
In the space of the glory the stresses of power contend;
through the kingdom my heart's revolutions ascribe to the
    power
quicken the backward wings of passages and paths.

Once, when the Prophet's shout had taken Cordova,
north I rode through a moon of Spanish winter,
and lay for a night in a lodging of ancient Israel,
twins of Levi, under the height of Monsalvat.

Sea-grey was one and sea-wrinkled,
one burned sun-black, with clawed hands;
guttural, across the charcoal fire, their chant
dropped into pauses, poured into channelled names.

The first mathematics of Ispahan trembled
before the intoned formulæ; their smiles cast
totals from a myriad intricate calculations,
while the screams of eagles in conflict shook the Sierras.

I sat and heard, aloof in my young seed-mail,
scornful of my secret attention; the hut shook,
the air span, with titles of cherubim and seraphim;
the voices rose into clearness; they pronounced *Netzach*.

Sharply I shouted into the sound : *Netzach ?*
What is Netzach ? Together and deeply they answered :
Netzach is the name of the Victory in the Blessing :
For the Lord created all things by means of his Blessing.

One now, sea-grey and wave-wrinkled,
calls through all my body to the sun-blackened :
The Lord created all things by means of his Blessing,
and they float upwards ; the paths open between.

Once the paths were interminable ; paths were stations.
Unangelical speed loitered upon them,
supposing the everlasting habitations had received it ;
only the dolphin Dinadan swam and smiled.

Then Iseult was living ; then was the tournament ;
then I longed, feared, fought, was angry.
Now if still I fight, fear, am angry,
I know those terminable paths are only paths.

Loneliest of lords, Dinadan smiled ; I feared.
Now no sound is near but aerial screams,
no soft voices, nothing except the harsh
scream of the eagle approaching the plateau of Netzach :

its scream and its passage approaching its primal station
backwards ; about me a scintillation of points,
points of the eagle's plumes, plumes that are paths ;
paths and plumes swoop to the unbelieved symbol.

I left the Prophet ; I lost Iseult ; I failed
to catch the beast out of Broceliande ;
Lancelot forgave me ; if I was christened in that pardon
it was half because I was a greater fool so.

I have gone back, down the road of Logres, the arm
of Iseult, the pass of Monsalvat, into the hut ;
I sit with the old men, as they were ; we sing :
The Lord created all things by means of his Blessing.

I utter the formula ; the formula is all that lives :
sharply the Prophet, Iseult, Lancelot, Dinadan,
call to me this at my dying, and I to them :
The Lord created all things by means of his Blessing.

If this is the kingdom, the power, the glory, my heart
formally offers the kingdom, endures the power,
joins to itself the aerial scream of the eagle . . .
That Thou only canst be Thou only art.

Percivale at Carbonek

In the rent saffron sun hovered the Grail.
Galahad stood in the arch of Carbonek;
the people of Pelles ran to meet him.
His eyes were sad: he sighed for Lancelot's pardon.

Joy remembered joylessness; joy kneeled
under the arch where Lancelot ran in frenzy.
The astonished angels of the spirit heard him moan:
Pardon, lord; pardon and bless me, father.

Doubtfully stood the celestial myrmidons, scions
of unremitted beauty; bright feet paused.
Aching with the fibrous infelicity of time,
pierced his implacability, Galahad kneeled.

The passage through Carbonek was short to the house of
    the Grail;
the wounded king waited for health; motionless
the subdued glory implored the kingdom
    to pardon its power and the double misery of Logres.

Under the arch the Merciful Child
wept for the grief of his father in reconciliation;
who was betrayed there by Merlin and Brisen
    to truth; he saw not; he was false to Guinevere.

G

Between the Infant and Bors and myself on each hand
under the arch I heard the padding of paws,
woven between us, and the faint howl of the wolf.
　　The High Prince shivered in the cold of bleak conjunction.

His hand shook ;　pale were his cheeks ;
his head the head of a skull, flesh
cleaving to bone ;　his dry voice rattled ;
　　' Pardon, Lord Lancelot ;　pardon and blessing, father.'

He knelt silent among the circles of the wolf.
Until the lover of Guinevere acknowledged his son
a bitter frost crept in the bones of Galahad.
　　The Host in the Lateran lay in a hid sepulchre.

Stiffly the Child's head turned ;　the drawn engine
slewed to his left, to Bors the kin of Lancelot.
He said ' Cousin, can you bear pardon
　　to the house of Carbonek from the fallen house of Camelot ? '

Bors answered :　' What should we forgive ? '
' Forgive Us,' the High Prince said, ' for Our existence ;
forgive the means of grace and the hope of glory.
　　In the name of Our father forgive Our mother for Our
　　birth.'

' Sir,' Bors said, ' only God forgives.
My lord Sir Lancelot my cousin is a lover and kind.
I assent to all, as I pray that my children assent
　　and through God join with me in bidding their birth.'

The Infant said : ' Go, cousin.' Bors
stepped from the arch ; the angelic household met him.
The High Prince stepped in his footprints ; into the sun
Galahad followed Bors ; Carbonek was entered.

The Last Voyage

The hollow of Jerusalem was a ship.

In the hall of Empire, on the right wall from the stair,
Solomon was painted, a small city and temple
rose beyond, reaching the level of his knee ;
all on a deck floated in a sea of dolphins.
His right hand, blessing, whelmed the djinn
who sank impotently around and drowned in the waters.
Rigid his left arm stretched to the queen Balkis ;
where her mouth on his hand tasted effectual magic,
intellectual art arm-fasted to the sensuous.
Solomon was the grand master of all creaturely being
in sublime necromancy, the rule and road of seeing
for those who have no necessity of existence in themselves ;
On the opposite wall, in a laureate ceremony,
Virgil to Taliessin stretched a shoot
of hazel—the hexameter, the decasyllabic line—
fetched from Homer beyond him ; by the king's poet
were the poets of Logres, Britain, and the ninefold isles :
the isles floated beyond them in a sea of dolphins.
But the actual ship, the hollow of Jerusalem,
beyond the shapes of empire, the capes of Carbonek,
over the topless waves of trenched Broceliande,
drenched by the everlasting spray of existence,
with no mind's sail reefed or set, no slaves at the motived oars,
drove into and clove the wind from unseen shores.
Swept from all altars, swallowed in a path of power

by the wrath that wrecks the pirates in the Narrow Seas,
now in the confidence of the charge, the thrust of the trust,
seizing the sea-curve, the shortest way between points,
to the point of accumulated distance, the safe tension
in each allotted joint of the knotted web of empire,
multiple without dimension, indivisible without uniformity,
the ship of Solomon (blessed be he) drove on.

Fierce in the prow the alchemical Infant burned,
red by celerity now conceiving the white;
behind him the folded silver column of Percivale,
hands on the royal shoulders, closed wings of flight,
inhaled the fine air of philosophical amazement;
Bors, mailed in black, completing the trine,
their action in Logres, kneeling on the deck to their right,
the flesh of fatherhood, unique as they in the Will,
prayed still for the need and the bliss of his household.
By three ways of exchange the City sped to the City;
against the off-shore wind that blew from Sarras
the ship and the song flew.

An infinite flight of doves from the storming sky
of Logres—strangely sea-travellers when the land melts—
forming to overfeather and overwhelm the helm,
numerous as men in the empire, the empire riding
the skies of the ocean, guiding by modulated stresses
on each spoke of the helm the vessel from the realm of Arthur,
lifted oak and elm to a new-ghosted power.
The hosted wings trapped the Infant's song;
blown back, tossed down, thrown
along the keel, the song hastening the keel

along the curve of the sea-way, the helm fastening
the whole ship to the right balance of the stresses ;
as the fine fair arm of pine-changed Cymodocea,
striking from the grey-green waters of tossed Tiber,
thrust the worshipful duke to the rescue of Rome ;
as the arm of the queen, finger-latched to Solomon's,
matched power to purpose and passion to peace.
The wonder that snapped once in the hollow of Jerusalem
was retrieved now along the level of the bulwark
to where the hands of Galahad were reeved on the prow :
the hollow of Jerusalem was within the hollow of his
    shoulders,
the ban and blessing of the empire ran in his arms,
from his feet the deck spread that was fleet on the sea.
The ship of Solomon (blessed be he) drove on.

Before the helm the ascending-descending sun
lay in quadrilateral covers of a saffron pall
over the bier and the pale body of Blanchefleur,
mother of the nature of lovers, creature of exchange ;
drained there of blood by the thighed wound,
she died another's death, another lived her life.
Where it was still to-night, in the last candles of Logres,
a lady danced, to please the sight of her friends ;
her cheeks were stained from the arteries of Percivale's
    sister.
Between them they trod the measure of heaven and earth,
and the dead woman waited the turn and throe of the dance
where, rafting and undershafting the quadruplicate sacrum,
below the saffron pall, the joyous woe of Blanchefleur,
the ship of Solomon (blessed be he) drove on.

Dinadan was lord of something more than irony,
he died in the deep schismatic war, when Gawaine
hewed the Table in twain, by a feud with his fellows
making peace with his doctrine : he pursued Lancelot
for the Throne's honour, by a side-path with his own.
His brother Agravaine caught the king's dolphin
on the sea-shore, in a track of the bewildered wood,
when by an ambush Lamorack was shot in the back
by the sons of the queen Morgause who slew their mother,
to clean their honour's claws in the earth of her body.
They drew Dinadan to broil on a bed of coals ;
their souls were glad to destroy the pertinence of curiosity ;
the merciful heaven drove the thick smoke to choke him.
But the Infant's song was thick with a litany of names
from the king and the king's friend to the least of the slaves.
He was borne through the waves to his end on a cry of
        substitution.
When he uttered Agravaine's name a light low
covered with flame the spread saffron veil ;
the heart of the dead Dinadan burned on the sun,
and gathered and fled through the air to the head of Percivale,
flew and flamed and flushed the argentine column.
The ship of Solomon (blessed be he) drove on.

Through the sea of omnipotent fact rushed the act of Galahad.
He glowed white ; he leaned against the wind
down the curved road among the topless waters.
He sang *Judica te, Deus* ; the wind,
driven by doves' wings along the arm-taut keel,
sang against itself *Judica te, Deus*.
Prayer and irony had said their say and ceased ;

the sole speech was speed.
In the hollow of Jerusalem the quadrilateral of the sun
was done on the deck beyond Broceliande.
In the monstrum of triangular speed,
in a path of lineal necessity,
the necessity of being was communicated to the son of
        Lancelot.
The ship and the song drove on.

In Logres the King's friend landed, Lancelot of Gaul.
Taliessin at Canterbury met him with the news
of Arthur's death and the overthrow of Mordred.
At the hour of the healing of Pelles
the two kings were one, by exchange of death and healing.
Logres was withdrawn to Carbonek ; it became Britain.

Taliessin at Lancelot's Mass

I came to his altar when dew was bright on the grass ;
he—he was not sworn of the priesthood—began the Mass.
The altar was an ancient stone laid upon stones ;
Carbonek's arch, Camelot's wall, frame of Bors' bones.

In armour before the earthen footpace he stood ;
on his surcoat the lions of his house, dappled with blood,
rampant, regardant ; but he wore no helm or sword,
and his hands were bare as Lateran's to the work of our Lord.

In the ritual before the altar Lancelot began to pass ;
all the dead lords of the Table were drawn from their graves
    to the Mass ;
they stood, inward turned, as shields on a white rushing deck,
between Nimue of Broceliande and Helayne of Carbonek.

In Blanchefleur's cell at Almesbury the queen Guinevere
felt the past exposed ; and the detail, sharp and dear,
draw at the pang in the breast till, rich and reconciled,
the mystical milk rose in the mother of Logres' child.

Out of the queen's substitution the wounded and dead king
entered into salvation to serve the holy Thing ;
singly seen in the Mass, owning the double Crown,
going to the altar Pelles, and Arthur moving down.

Lancelot and Arthur wove the web ; the sky
opened on moon and sun ; between them, light-traced on
    high,
the unseen knight of terror stood as a friend ;
invisible things and visible waited the end.

Lancelot came to the Canon ; my household stood
around me, bearers of the banners, bounteous in blood ;
each at the earthen footpace ordained to be blessed and to
    bless,
each than I and than all lordlier and less.

Then at the altar We sang in Our office the cycle of names
of their great attributed virtues ; the festival of flames
fell from new sky to new earth ; the light in bands
of bitter glory renewed the imperial lands.

Then the Byzantine ritual, the Epiclesis, began ;
then their voices in Ours invoked the making of man ;
petal on petal floated out of the blossom of the Host,
and all ways the Theotokos conceived by the Holy Ghost.

We exposed, We exalted the Unity ; prismed shone
web, paths, points ; as it was done
the antipodean zones were retrieved round a white rushing
    deck,
and the Acts of the Emperor took zenith from Caucasia to
    Carbonek.

Over the altar, flame of anatomized fire,
the High Prince stood, gyre in burning gyre ;
day level before him, night massed behind ;
the Table ascended ; the glories intertwined.

The Table ascended ; each in turn lordliest and least—
slave and squire, woman and wizard, poet and priest ;
interchanged adoration, interdispersed prayer,
the ruddy pillar of the Infant was the passage of the porphyry
     stair.

That which had been Taliessin rose in the rood ;
in the house of Galahad over the altar he stood,
manacled by the web, in the web made free ;
there was no capable song for the joy in me :

joy to new joy piercing from paths foregone ;
that which had been Taliessin made joy to a Joy unknown ;
manifest Joy speeding in a Joy unmanifest.
Lancelot's voice below sang : *Ite ; missa est.*

Fast to the Byzantine harbour gather the salvaged sails ;
that which was once Taliessin rides to the barrows of Wales
up the vales of the Wye ; if skill be of work or of will
in the dispersed homes of the household, let the Company
     pray for it still.

NOTE

NOTE

These references are not intended to help the poems as poems. All that comes from Malory is, I think, familiar, but though he provided many hints in his images he does not seem to trouble to work out the possibilities of relation. I have summarized a few as they are used here, and made what other acknowledgements are due.

Title.] This was not taken from Tennyson, but it was confirmed later by a line in *The Holy Grail* :

> Taliessin is our fullest throat of song.

pp. 3 and 4.] The images in the third and fourth stanzas are those used of a particular state of being in *Comus*, the *Nightingale Ode*, the *Prelude*, and the *Divine Comedy*.

pp. 15 et seq.] Bors was the nephew of Lancelot, and the companion of Galahad and Percivale. He had two children by Elayne, the daughter of King Brangoris, ' and sauf for her syre Bors was a clene mayden '.

pp. 20 et seq.] Lamorack was the brother of Percivale and Blanchefleur. He was the lover of the queen Morgause of Orkney, Arthur's sister. The two were killed by her sons, Gawaine and Agravaine, for the honour of the house of Orkney.

pp. 39–41.] After the dolorous blow struck against King Pelles in Carbonek by Balin the Savage, Balin and Balan his brother killed each other unknowingly, and Arthur unknowingly committed incest with his sister Morgause, who became by him the mother of Mordred.

p. 45.] The quotation from Heracleitus was taken from Mr. Yeats's book, *A Vision*.

p. 56.] ' the feeling intellect ' is from the *Prelude*, Book 14.

p. 69.] Galahad came to Caerleon after Palomides had been christened on the Feast of Pentecost. ' In the honour of the hyghness of Galahad he was ledde in to kinge Arthurs chamber and there rested in his own bedde '—*Morte d'Arthur*, Book XIII. The image of the stone and shell is from the *Prelude*, Book 5.

p. 75.] The variation of the Merlin tale is due to Swinburne (but this Merlin is young): *Tristram of Lyonesse*, Books 1 and 6.

p. 78.] Netzach is a station on the Sephirotic Tree ; its quality is Victory.

p. 86.] Blanchefleur died from a letting of blood to heal a sick lady ; her body was taken by the three lords of the quest, and buried 'in the spyrytual place'.

p. 90.] 'the unseen knight' was Garlon, the brother of King Pelles. It was through the quarrel with him that Balin the Savage came to strike the dolorous blow at Pelles 'with the same spere that Longeus smote oure lord to the hearte', so that 'he myght never be hole tyl Galahad the haute prince heled him in the quest of the Sangraille.'

Printed in Great Britain by Butler & Tanner Ltd., Frome and London

1.48